2021

John dear,

Such fond memories of
same old stamping grounds)
with you. Those were the days!

Much love,
Dolly

IMAGES
of America

WINNETKA

Originally located on the grounds of the Indian Hill Club, the Schmidt-Burnham House, the oldest log structure in Cook Country, was most likely built in 1837 by the Schmidt family of Koblenz, Germany, and is notable for being the only home in the area to be continuously inhabited for 165 years. It has been moved twice, once in 1917 by the artist Anita Willets Burnham and again in 2003 by the Winnetka Historical Society. In June 2005, the house was listed on the National Register of Historic Places. (Courtesy of Raymond Britt.)

On the cover: In 1962, these 13- and 14-year-old boys speed skate at the Winnetka Park District's outdoor skate park in the Hubbard Woods neighborhood of Winnetka. (Courtesy of the Winnetka Park District.)

IMAGES
of America

WINNETKA

ArLynn Leiber Presser

ARCADIA
PUBLISHING

Published by Arcadia Publishing
Charleston, South Carolina

Library of Congress Control Number: 2008942895

For all general information contact Arcadia Publishing at:
Telephone 843-853-2070
Fax 843-853-0044
E-mail sales@arcadiapublishing.com
For customer service and orders:
Toll-Free 1-888-313-2665

Visit us on the Internet at www.arcadiapublishing.com

*Winnetka is a town of good neighbors—thank you,
neighbors, for being so good to me!*

CONTENTS

ACKNOWLEDGMENTS

I am grateful to Chief Joseph DeLopez, Sgt. James Harrison, and Glenn Florkow of the Winnetka Police Department; Karen Marousek of the Hadley School for the Blind; Katie Macica and Patti Van Cleave of the Winnetka Historical Society; Tura Cottingham of North Shore Country Day School; Mary Cherveny of the Winnetka Park District; Anne O'Malley of New Trier High School; the staff of Phototronics; Joseph and Eastman Presser for their patience; Maximillian for his support; Tom Bulger; Dennis Sears; and the Britt family for its encouragement and the use of its private collection.

INTRODUCTION

As so many villages and cities do, Winnetka started as a place to stop along the way to someplace else. The Green Bay Trail was originally a means for the Native American tribes to travel north and south along the shore of Lake Michigan. European Americans used the arduous 500-mile trail to link Fort Dearborn (Chicago) and Fort Howard (Wisconsin). In the worst winter conditions, the trip took a full month. An enterprising family from Vermont built a cabin and a tavern for weary travelers. Four years later, the first hotel—for men only—was built. A blacksmith shop opened to service the horses and stagecoaches that passed. A stagecoach made the tavern part of its regular route, and, without any intention, the place that was just a stop along the way became a place to live, to raise children, to worship, to join hands as neighbors.

The name Winnetka was settled upon in 1854. Charles Peck was platting land in anticipation of the building of the Chicago and Milwaukee Railroad. Charles and his wife Sarah were friends with the Evans family, which had recently lent its name to the new village Evanston. Mrs. Evans was particularly adamant that the Pecks name the area Peckville. But Charles's wife Sarah had other ideas. She had recently read a book on Native Americans of the area, and she said that the new village would be named Winnetka, meaning "beautiful land" in the Native American language.

Although there is neither record of the book she read nor any evidence of the term in any Native American tongue, there is no doubt that Winnetka lives up to its moniker. It boasts tall, stately oak trees and graceful waving hostas. Look to the east and there is Lake Michigan, glittering in the sun. To the west is a forest preserve. People who stayed devised a town. They built businesses, churches, and schools.

They were independent-minded people, quick to figure out new solutions to old problems. They were educational pioneers, determined to make education available to every child and to making that education meaningful. The innovations of the Winnetka schools have transformed the way Americans think about schools.

Winnetkans were aware of the privilege that came with living in such a community—and when the call for arms was heard, they were the first to respond. They have lost sons (and one daughter) in overseas conflicts, but they never shrink from duty. And Winnetkans serve others in peacetime, with charitable clubs and organizations that somehow make doing good feel good.

Winnetka has faced its share of tragedy. In 1860, the side-wheel steamer *Lady Elgin* was struck by a small schooner off the coast of Highland Park, just north of Winnetka. The survivors who reached land in Winnetka were treated in homes that became makeshift hospitals. In 1884, village president James L. Willson and his wife were brutally murdered and the crime was never solved. In 1903, the village lost one family to fire at the Iroquois Theater. In 1988, Laurie Dann entered the Hubbard Woods Elementary School and shot six students, killing young second grader Nick Corwin. She killed herself in a home across the street from the school, after holding a family hostage and shooting one of its members. And, of course, there are those who have made the ultimate sacrifice for their country.

Each time tragedy strikes, Winnetkans somehow find a way to make something good become the lasting memory. When the Fox family was killed at the Iroquois Theater, a church was built for the community in its honor. When Nick Corwin was killed, a park was named for him.

Winnetka is a small suburb—under 15,000 residents—just 20 miles north of Chicago. It has three public elementary schools and two public middle schools and is home to New Trier High School. Two parochial schools, one independent private school, and many preschools round out the educational opportunities. Winnetka has five public beaches and a host of well-maintained parks. It boasts two golf courses, one private and one public. To the west is a forest preserve and quiet lagoons upon which one can canoe. It is beautiful in its aspect, but it is also beautiful in the way its residents are good neighbors and good friends to one another.

One

A PLACE ALONG
THE WAY

In 1832, Congress established the Green Bay Trail as a post road linking Fort Dearborn in what is now known as Chicago with Fort Howard, a U.S. Army fortification in Green Bay, Wisconsin. On the trail, the traveler would welcome a tavern, a hotel, and a place to reshoe a horse. Winnetka served as just that place along the way for many years.

But the bare necessities for the weary traveler meant that some people settled. And when they settled down, they wanted a community—a church, a school, a general store. A village was formed and families counted the generations who have stayed. While the Winnetka population was a mere 100 people in 1850, the village swelled with new residents after the Chicago and Milwaukee Railroad (C&M) was built to augment the trail in 1854 and again when the Great Chicago Fire displaced so many families in 1871. By the end of the century, Winnetka was a town of close to 2,000 people with its own traditions, innovations, and customs. It had become someplace to stay.

C. E. ROGERS, Fond du Lac, Wis.

Postman Alexis Clermont traveled on foot from Fort Dearborn to Fort Howard and back to deliver the mail. The 500-mile round-trip journey could take as long as a month in winter. During the summer months, the mail was delivered by sailing vessels. Although a treaty was in place with local tribes, over 100 postmen were said to have lost their lives at the hands of Native Americans. (Courtesy of the Winnetka Historical Society.)

The Indian Trail Tree grew in what is now Fuller Lane in south Winnetka. The tree was said to have been bent by Native Americans in 1770 in order to give directions to travelers between present-day Chicago and Green Bay, Wisconsin. There is evidence—bones, arrowheads, and pottery shards—that the dominant tribe of the area, the Potawatomi, frequented a campsite near the present-day Indian Hills Club, a mile to the west of the tree. (Courtesy of the Winnetka Historical Society.)

PATTERSON TAVERN

In 1833, the Treaty of Chicago was signed and the Potawatomi, Chippewa, and Ottawa tribes were moved to land west of the Mississippi River. Pioneers rushed into what was now regarded as safe territory. In 1836, Erastus Patterson, his wife Zernah, and their children—Olive, Moses, Azel, Joseph, and Lucia—left Vermont and settled in what would become Winnetka and built a tavern for Green Bay Trail travelers. Business was good, and stagecoach service was established in the same year. Erastus and 12-year-old Lucia died in 1837. (Courtesy of the Winnetka Historical Society.)

Zernah Patterson, already 42 years old when the family settled in Winnetka, continued to run the tavern with her remaining children's help. Ten years later, daughter Olive married and moved with her husband to Milwaukee. Moses and Azel headed west, lured by the stories of the gold rush. The tavern was sold to John Garland in 1847 and torn down 10 years later. Zernah remained in Winnetka, and here she sits for a final portrait with three members of her family. (Courtesy of the Winnetka Historical Society.)

In 1843, John Happ, his wife Gertrude, and their nine children came from Trier, Germany, to open the first blacksmith shop in what would become the central business district in Winnetka. There were so many families from Trier settling in the area that in 1850 the township of which Winnetka is part was named New Trier. John and Gertrude's grandson John P. Happ (second from left) must have felt right at home sitting in the Brady Blacksmith Shop in this 1925 picture. (Courtesy of the Winnetka Historical Society.)

Charles Peck, together with his friend Walter Gurnee, president of the C&M, platted the original subdivision of Winnetka in 1854. That same year, the C&M came through Winnetka. The Peck home has since been torn down, but the home site is still a Winnetka landmark. This rendering of the home was made into a Christmas card by the Dovenmuehle greeting card company. The Pecks donated to the young village the parcel of land known as the Winnetka Village Green. (Courtesy of the Winnetka Historical Society.)

Artemas Carter, a real estate and lumber trade businessman, was the first village president and served from 1869 to 1873. When he took office, the population of Winnetka was 450. The Great Chicago Fire drove many people from their homes, and, in considering a place to start over, many people chose Winnetka, swelling the population over the next 10 years. Carter served four terms as village president and guided the village from being a little dot on the map to being a place some could call their hometown. (Courtesy of the Winnetka Historical Society.)

Helen Hubbard was sister to Artemas Carter's wife Anna. Helen and Gilbert Hubbard purchased property near Winnetka's lakeside train station in the north part of the village after the Great Chicago Fire destroyed their home. Their land became known as Hubbard Woods, and the train station was later renamed the Hubbard Woods station. (Courtesy of the Winnetka Historical Society.)

In 1884, village president James L. Willson and his bedridden wife Mary were killed in their home at 688 Cherry Street. Mary was slashed with the very sword that had been a lasting memento of their only son George, who had died of yellow fever while fighting in the Civil War. The crime was never solved. Here a picture taken the day after the murders features the stained bedding and blood-splattered walls of Mary's room. (Courtesy of the Winnetka Historical Society.)

The young village required horses for travel and, of course, an undertaker for the dead. Fred Richardson's livery shop was located near John Happ's blacksmith shop and shared space with the Schaefer Brothers Undertakers. (Courtesy of the Winnetka Historical Society.)

Everett Osgood opened an office to help villagers with their real estate transactions. He also sold insurance and made house and business loans. His father, Stacy Whitney Osgood, served as village president from 1892 to 1894 and as Winnetka's postmaster. Everett Osgood also worked as the village's postmaster. (Courtesy of the Winnetka Historical Society.)

In this 1893 photograph, a settee is ready for delivery from the H. A. Lindwall Upholstering shop. The business thrived and moved to a bigger building when the village purchased the land to build the Winnetka Village Hall. Linked to Chicago by a railway just steps from their homes, Winnetkans of prominence in Chicago business make their homes in Winnetka. (Courtesy of the Winnetka Historical Society.)

Robert Moth opened a general store in 1875 on the corner of Elm Street and Green Bay Road, across from the Winnetka train station. The store carried groceries, dry goods, hardware, and feed. Max Meyer and John Gage purchase the store in 1882 and at one time shared the space with Dr. J. W. Nelson, a surgeon, and Winnetka's first public telephone station. (Courtesy of the Winnetka Historical Society.)

After purchasing the store, Max Meyer expanded the business to include the freshly formed Bank of M. K. Meyer. In 1912, a fire destroyed much of the store, and Meyer decided to concentrate on banking instead of retail sales. Meyer later named the bank Winnetka Trust and Savings Bank. (Courtesy of the Winnetka Historical Society.)

Max and Nellie Meyer sit for a portrait in 1893. In addition to buying the general store from Robert Moth, Max had married Moth's daughter Nellie. When the Winnetka Community House first began showing moving pictures in 1911, Max was in charge of selecting the pictures to be shown. A ticket cost 5¢, and, because of their novelty, patrons did not mind being surprised by his selections, which generally ran toward adventures and westerns. (Courtesy of the Winnetka Historical Society.)

Winnetka's first public school was built in 1859 with private funds. One of its first students was Kate Dwyer, who would go on to a 48-year career as a teacher in the village. In 1884, she poses with her students at Academy Hall. Academy Hall was built in 1870 and was used over the years as a village hall, a police department, a fire department, and a library. It was torn down in 1964 to make room for the new public safety building. (Courtesy of the Winnetka Historical Society.)

Fires as far north as Winnetka and south as Evanston were battled by these members of the Lakeside Hose Company. The private company was located in what was then called the Lakeside neighborhood (later called Hubbard Woods). John Taylor (first row, right) was father to Harold Taylor (second row, center), who would have been called a "junior member" of the company. (Courtesy of the Winnetka Historical Society.)

In 1902, Winnetka created a combination professional-volunteer fire department. The fire marshal was paid $50 per year as a salary, and professional members were given a $2 honorarium for each fire call. In 1993, the fire department became a fully professional department, complete with emergency medical personnel. The police and fire department share headquarters at the public safety building on Green Bay Road. (Courtesy of the Winnetka Historical Society.)

Winnetka flourished at the dawn of the 20th century, and these young daughters of businessman Jay Woodward Powers had a more comfortable life. Violet, Lily, and Lydia Powers, from left to right, pose for a portrait in their home at 1002 Vine Street. Violet would become one of the first women doctors in Chicago. (Courtesy of the Winnetka Historical Society.)

Winnetka had its share of eccentrics. John Busscher lived in a small house near the corner of Green Bay and Willow Roads. One of his interests was in spiritualism, a highly popular subject in the 1890s. His portrait includes a gathering of spirits around his head. (Courtesy of the Winnetka Historical Society.)

Village marshal John Coutre patrolled the village on a motorized bicycle during his tenure from 1909 to 1912. Village marshals during the 19th century generally served one-year terms, but the position of village marshal was eliminated in 1950 with responsibilities divided between a village manager, village engineer, police chief, and fire chief. (Courtesy of the Winnetka Police Department.)

Winnetka's police department hired its first woman, Gertrude Thurston, as a juvenile officer in 1917. She was one of the original founders of the Winnetka Woman's Club and also served as a New Trier Township trustee. Here she poses with the police force, including village marshal Waino Peterson at far right. She retired in 1945. (Courtesy of the Winnetka Police Department.)

Winnetka's police department was one of the first to hire African Americans. In 1914, officer Jerry Cross poses for his official portrait. It was highly unusual for any police department to employ African Americans as officers and yet, officer Cross commanded respect and admiration in the community. Today the Winnetka Police Department keeps a photograph of all past and present officers on file, but none could be so strikingly handsome as this. (Courtesy of the Winnetka Police Department.)

In the late 19th and early 20th century, Winnetka maintained a cadet corps and a girls' auxiliary corps. The corps served as the equivalent of today's ROTC and stressed preparedness for war and other emergencies. Later the cadet corps would be organized at New Trier High School and would replace the two groups. Julian Buckbee, second from left in this picture, went on to serve in the Spanish-American War. (Courtesy of the Winnetka Historical Society.)

Ice for preserving food as well as water for table use were delivered to homes and businesses. John McFarlin opened the first ice delivery company, but there was enough business in town to support several ice companies. The North Shore Ice Company was located on the northernmost edge of town. Here two deliverymen take a break from their duties to pose for a picture. (Courtesy of the Winnetka Historical Society.)

Rev. Quincy L. Dowd of the village's Congregational church helped organize the Village Improvement Association. One of his greatest contributions to Winnetka was the "town meeting" of 1890, which he organized with the help of Henry Demarest Lloyd. The annual meetings were intended to be uplifting, often including music and sometimes readings from papers such as "Modern Socialism" and "The Reform of Criminals." Only gradually did these meetings focus on village affairs. (Courtesy of the Winnetka Historical Society.)

Reverend Dowd's wife Nellie was herself involved in the village. She toured the village on her carriage, visiting shut-ins and the sick. She founded neighborhood circles—clubs organized around a particular street or neighborhood. The clubs were meant to introduce newly settled women to the customs of the community. (Courtesy of the Winnetka Historical Society.)

Publisher Henry Demarest Lloyd and Reverend Dowd envisioned the development of what is now called the caucus system—a nonpartisan system in which representatives from every neighborhood would come together to make important decisions and appointments. With its adoption in 1915, political battles over appointments to village positions have been largely avoided. (Courtesy of the Winnetka Historical Society.)

Even as Winnetka became an affluent community, it still maintained a forward-thinking attitude. Henry Demarest Lloyd, nicknamed the "Socialist Millionaire" in the press of the day, was a conscience of the community. A statue on the grounds of his home the Wayside is inscribed with three Lloyd quotations, including "Society should give every man not his daily bread but a chance to earn his daily bread." (Courtesy of the Winnetka Historical Society.)

The Wayside was the site of many meetings of activists and community organizers, including those committed to obtaining the freedom of those accused of murder in the infamous Haymarket Riots. Henry Demarest Lloyd believed in equality, and on the statue outside his home is inscribed, "No tenements for some and castles for others." The Wayside was designated a national historic landmark in 1976. (Courtesy of the Winnetka Historical Society.)

A water tower, 119 feet high, was built on the lakefront at the east end of Tower Road in 1893. The tower stored up to 46,000 gallons of water and allowed Winnetkans running water in their homes and businesses. Over the years, the water tower became the iconic Winnetka image, and residents could walk up to its balcony to look east to Lake Michigan or south to the Wayside. It was torn down in 1972, when high-pressure tanks were put in. (Courtesy of the Winnetka Historical Society.)

Emilie Hoyt Fox was the picture of happiness at her wedding in the 1880s. Scant years later, she would meet a tragic end when she took her children to see a Christmas season production of *Mr. Bluebeard* at the Iroquois Theater in Chicago. (Courtesy of the Winnetka Historical Society.)

At the December 30, 1903, production of *Mr. Bluebeard* at the Iroquois Theater, Winnetka resident Emilie Lydia Fox was killed when the stage caught fire. Her brothers George Sidney and Willis Hoyt, as well as their mother, Emilie, also perished. Over 600 theater patrons—mostly women and children on holiday—died within 20 minutes of the initial sighting of the flames. Emily's grandfather William Hoyt built the Christ Church building in memory of his loss. (Courtesy of the Winnetka Historical Society.)

The Lacay family horse Tinker Bell poses for a photograph in 1909, the same year James Pugh bought the first automobile to be used in Winnetka. (Courtesy of the Winnetka Historical Society.)

With the introduction of the automobile came the need for police to monitor speeding traffic. Rope strung across the street as a type of roadblock served as a deterrent to speeders, as demonstrated by village marshal Henry Leach and officer John Dehmlous. (Courtesy of the Winnetka Police Department.)

Early Winnetka residents were often German immigrants—many from John Happ's hometown of Trier. These Winnetkans brought with them their German traditions, including the Christmas tree. Here the Boldenweck children and their friends gather around the *Tannenbaum*, thinking perhaps of St. Nicholas's imminent arrival. (Courtesy of the Winnetka Historical Society.)

Winnetkans made sure they had opportunities for fun. Here these men from the Winnetka Men's Baseball Club pose for the 1893 season team picture. Note the quilted pants of the catcher (third from left, back row) The baseball club played other North Shore village teams. (Courtesy of the Winnetka Historical Society.)

Winnetka in winter was and is a wonderful place to be a child. In 1897, these children brought out their sleds on the hills in the Hubbard Woods neighborhood. Even though their parents were there to keep an eye on them, they still managed to have fun. (Courtesy of the Winnetka Historical Society.)

Eric Nelson and Elizabeth Gursteers sit for a wedding portrait in April 1899. With his brothers, Nelson founded the North Shore Laundry, which cleaned and pressed the suits, linens, and dresses of Winnetka residents—such a business signaled the town's prosperity. He was also a cofounder of the nondenominational Winnetka Bible Church. (Courtesy of the Winnetka Historical Society.)

Constance Tyrrell, daughter of Frederick S. Tyrrell (one of the first donors to the Winnetka Community House), married Jack Ritchie in 1912. In 1932, when the Winnetka Community House was being rebuilt after a massive fire, Constance made a generous donation to the rebuilding campaign, and the Frederick S. Tyrrell conference room was named for her father. (Courtesy of the Winnetka Historical Society.)

The Winnetka Community House was opened in 1911 on land donated by Douglas Smith. These children are part of a theatrical presentation on the grounds of the house in 1915. Their fancy 18th-century costumes seem to have impressed upon their young minds the seriousness of their thespian endeavors. (Courtesy of the Winnetka Historical Society.)

The Winnetka Community House boasted a gymnasium that was modestly equipped so as to allow imaginative play by children. It was, however, laid out for use as a basketball and tennis court, as well as a baseball diamond. The 1911 gymnastics team poses for this photograph. (Courtesy of the Winnetka Historical Society.)

From the beginning, the Winnetka Community House provided a variety of programs. In 1915, there were over 75 organizations using the facilities. Here a lithe instructor trains young boys in dance. The gymnasium gallery allowed parents to observe their children. (Courtesy of the Winnetka Historical Society.)

The Winnetka Community House became a center of community life. Much of the building was destroyed in a fire in 1930, well after this picture was taken. It was repaired and rebuilt with private funds, an extraordinary achievement during the Great Depression. (Courtesy of the Winnetka Historical Society.)

Here at the Winnetka Village Green, from left to right, officers Joseph Pikarski, John Dehmlow, Theodore Flynn, Waino Peterson, and Fred Winter pose for a picture as they attend Memorial Day services in the early 1900s. The Winnetka Village Green was donated to the village in 1869 by Charles Peck and became the center of town festivities, celebrations, and remembrances. Both Flynn and Peterson would go on to become village marshals. (Courtesy of the Winnetka Police Department.)

The Winnetka Police Department was once housed in Academy Hall. Here village marshal Waino Peterson (seventh from the left) stands with his men. Between 1920 and 1930, the population of Winnetka nearly doubled from 6,694 to 12,219, and the police department faced the challenges of a bigger town. (Courtesy of the Winnetka Police Department.)

The Winnetka Village Hall was dedicated in 1926. The gracious Georgian Revival building was designed by Winnetka resident Edwin Clark, who also designed the administration building and primate house for the Lincoln Park Zoo as well as a number of North Shore homes. The cost of building the Winnetka Village Hall—$240,000—was fully paid for through savings and revenue generated by village ownership of electrical and water utilities. (Courtesy of the Winnetka Historical Society.)

The Winnetka Village Hall today is the administrative center of town. It houses the council room where the village trustees meet to hear public matters. On the second floor are the offices of the village manager, an administrator who implements the directions of the trustees. He also serves as village clerk. (Courtesy of Raymond Britt.)

Two

EDUCATIONAL PIONEERS

Winnetka had all the elements in place as a wonderful place to live—beautiful houses, shops, a governmental system, and a ready police and fire department. But that was not enough to create a village. Parents wanted their children to have the best education possible.

In 1856, Sarah Peck opened a small private school in a home on Sheridan Road, but many parents could not afford the tuition. Still, the notion of universal public education was catching on around the country, and Winnetka was quick to see its wisdom.

Winnetka was a place for educational pioneers. Its public school educational philosophy has been called developmental or progressive. Its proponents argue that children need to develop at their own pace and can be educated through the guidance of their curiosity. Sometimes that has led to excesses—so-called creative spelling has sometimes worried parents that their children would not be prepared for the real world.

Still, Winnetka children thrive at New Trier High School—a public high school that serves the five towns of New Trier Township and is located in the southern tip of the village. New Trier High School students outscore other North Shore high schools on SAT and ACT tests, and these graduates go on to the finest colleges and universities.

Winnetka has a story that extends beyond the public schools. The town boasts two parochial schools as well as a half-dozen preschools and a correspondence school for the blind. It also is home to one of the country's premier country day schools.

At the corner of Elm Street and Maple Avenue, near the Happ blacksmith shop and on the present-day Winnetka Village Green, a one-room schoolhouse was built with private funds in 1859. Just 25 students were enrolled. The first year's budget was $200 to pay the teacher's salary and to buy fuel to heat the classroom. Turnover was high—there were five teachers over the next 10 years. (Courtesy of the Winnetka Historical Society.)

It was generally presumed that marriage meant the end of a woman's career. Ida (Stanley) Goss, wife of Charles Goss, poses for her wedding picture in 1880. She had been the principal of Winnetka's schools the previous year, and the expression captured by the photographer may suggest some ambivalence she might have felt about leaving her job. (Courtesy of the Winnetka Historical Society.)

In 1897, Fr. Frederick Haarth came to Winnetka to open the Sacred Heart Church. He established the Sacred Heart School in 1902. Fifty-four students enrolled and were taught by Franciscan nuns in a building adjoining the church. Father Haarth served 43 years in Winnetka. Today Winnetka has two parochial schools—Sacred Heart School and SS. Faith, Hope and Charity School. (Courtesy of the Winnetka Historical Society.)

In 1907, these kindergartners sit for story time at the Horace Mann School, which was built in 1899 and designed by Winnetka resident William Otis on the western side of the railroad tracks. The Horace Mann building was razed in 1940 to make way for a post office, public parking, and Dwyer Park (named for longtime teacher Kate Dwyer). Horace Mann was an educational reformer and congressman from Massachusetts who proposed a free and diverse public education. (Courtesy of the Winnetka Historical Society.)

This Horace Mann classroom might appear to be typical of a public school, but note the "grocery store" at the back of the room. The grocery store would have been operated by the students of the classroom with very little interference by teachers. This "learning by doing" was a forerunner to the progressive education movement. (Courtesy of the Winnetka Historical Society.)

Although Winnetka was progressive in its educational notions, there was some concern about allowing boys and girls to study together. Boys tended to lag behind academically, while the need for physical education was presumed to be greater for boys than girls. Some educators argued that the sexes should be educated separately, and they were in some subjects. Here girls work at a central station in a domestic science class at the Horace Mann School. (Courtesy of the Winnetka Historical Society.)

In 1911, renown municipal engineer Samuel S. Greeley suggested that students would be better served by a neighborhood school system, particularly since half the student body had to cross the railroad tracks in order to reach the Horace Mann School. (Courtesy of the Winnetka Historical Society.)

The school district built the Samuel S. Greeley School on the eastern side of the village for $45,000. It was designed by Winnetka residents William Otis and Edwin Clark. A color guard of Boy Scouts escorted Greeley from his home to the 1913 dedication ceremony. Speaking of the school, Greeley declared, "Good teachers come high, but believe me, no other stock on the list will pay such dividends." (Courtesy of Joseph Presser.)

In 1915, a new school was built on the north side of the village. Initially called the Skokie School, it boasted an auditorium and four classrooms, each with a skylight and its own outside entrance. In 1924, the school's name was changed to Hubbard Woods, in honor of the Hubbard family. In 1988, the school was to suffer an inexplicable tragedy—Laurie Dann would enter the school with firearms, wounding several students and killing second grader Nick Corwin before committing suicide at a home across the street from the school. (Courtesy of Raymond Britt.)

New Trier High School, designed by Normand S. Patten, opened in 1901 on Winnetka Avenue at the border of the village of Kenilworth. There were just 76 students and six faculty members when it opened in February during a bitter snowstorm. The curriculum included Latin, Greek, French, German, math, science, history, and freehand drawing. Extracurricular activities were not encouraged because it was supposed that students had chores to do at home. (Courtesy of New Trier High School.)

New Trier High School students and faculty gather in front of the building for this picture in 1902. Business courses and athletics were added to the curriculum that year; sewing and cooking were added in 1904, and the music department was organized in 1906. The school drew students from the entire New Trier Township—Winnetka, Kenilworth, Glencoe, Wilmette, and Northfield. (Courtesy of New Trier High School.)

New Trier High School teams were initially called Terriers or Green Waves (the school colors were and are blue and green). Today the teams are known as the Trevians, named for the German city Trier from which so many families immigrated. These Terriers played boys' heavyweight basketball in 1912. They practiced in an unfinished second-floor space that they shared with the other Terriers and Green Waves. (Courtesy of New Trier High School.)

In 1917, Virginia Buchanan, vice president of the New Trier High School Girls' Athletics Club, stands flanked by club president Roberta Skinner (left) and secretary Florence Pease. New Trier High School offered girls' physical education instruction and even had a modest tennis team. At the time, girls were prohibited from participating in the Illinois High School Athletics Association. (Courtesy of New Trier High School.)

Carleton Washburne was superintendent of the public schools from 1919 to 1943. He developed the Winnetka Plan of education, which expanded the school's focus to include the social and emotional development of the child. The plan emphasized the need to master essentials in academic subjects but allowed for students to develop beyond those essentials at their own pace. Here he inspects a student's work at a science exhibit. (Courtesy of the Winnetka Historical Society.)

North Shore Country Day School was founded by parents who were dissatisfied with the public school system but unwilling to send their children to boarding schools. The first headmaster, Perry Dunlap Smith, and Supt. Carleton Washburne had occupied adjoining desks at the Chicago Institute when they were young. In September 1919, Smith and Superintendent Washburne arrived in Winnetka, neither aware the other was coming. It was a surprising reunion—the two had last seen each other as classmates in a seventh grade taught by educational reformer Col. Francis Parker. (Courtesy of North Shore Country Day School.)

Supt. Carleton Washburne and Winnetka resident and patent attorney Theodore Hinton designed the first jungle gym in 1921. It was originally at the Horace Mann School but was moved to Crow Island School in 1940. A second jungle gym sits in the backyard of the Winnetka Historical Society Museum. It was first designed as a means to teach children the Cartesian system of coordinates, but children just liked to hang, swing, climb, and play on it. (Courtesy of the Winnetka Historical Society.)

At Winnetka's Hubbard Woods elementary school, a school play emphasizes the evils of mankind—suspicion, privilege, fear, greed, ignorance, intolerance, and selfishness. An eighth evil would have been part of the production, but its representative, Jeanette Nelson, had the measles and stayed home. Under Supt. Carleton Washburne's guidance, Winnetka schools emphasized character education as well as academics. (Courtesy of the Winnetka Historical Society.)

North Shore Country Day School operated almost like a boarding school in the sense that students stayed at the school all day, going to their homes for evening meals and to sleep. As established on the very first day of classes in 1919, mornings began with morning exercises, in which all members of the school community met for presentations by classes, individual students, faculty members, or outside speakers. Perry Dunlap Smith differed from Superintendent Washburne only insofar as he placed greater emphasis on rigorous academics. (Courtesy of North Shore Country Day School.)

Headmaster Smith had been a lineman on Harvard University's football team, and he considered athletics to be as important to the student as academics. At one point, he even filled in as fullback on the school's football team. North Shore Country Day School students are even today required to perform in a school play, complete a community service project, and participate in team sports. (Courtesy of North Shore Country Day School.)

Throughout the 1920s, North Shore Country Day School produced a yearly operetta. It has been observed that one could count on alumni to burst into W. S. Gilbert and Arthur Sullivan songs upon meeting one another. Headmaster Smith helped out by playing the bass in the orchestra pit. The school continued to produce high-quality theatrical productions even after the days of operettas were left behind. (Courtesy of North Shore Country Day School.)

49

While North Shore Country Day School was able to maintain small classes and a small community feel, New Trier High School was growing rapidly. Here the band of 1921–1922 poses with its director Joseph Schumacher (second row, center). The music department, begun in 1906, had rapidly expanded as new extracurricular clubs and sports gave every student a chance to participate. (Courtesy of New Trier High School.)

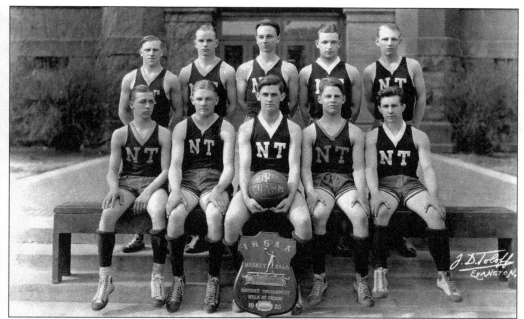

In 1923, these proud members of the New Trier High School boys' basketball team won the Illinois High School Athletics Association district tournament held in Cicero. New Trier High School's biggest conference rival in basketball is Evanston High School, and since 1981, the two games these schools play together each season are played at Northwestern University's arena. (Courtesy of New Trier High School.)

The New Trier High School senior class of 1924 sits for a portrait in front of the school. Supt. Frederic Clerk wisely created the advisory system that is still in place today—advisories are groups of boys and girls paired with teachers of the same sex. Advisories bond as a group for all four years, allowing for students to have at least one faculty member aware of their individual needs. Ability grouping (also known as leveling) places students with like abilities in the same classes. (Courtesy of New Trier High School.)

New Trier High School faculty members gather at the front of the building for a group portrait in 1925. The faculty had started with just six members and had expanded over the quarter century. The student population was close to 1,500. Although the campus had grown to 27 acres, the facilities were inadequate. (Courtesy of New Trier High School.)

In 1926, the New Trier High School marching band was led by Joseph Schumacher (front). Football had been tried unsuccessfully in 1908, and it was not until faculty member E. L. "Duke" Childs put together a team in 1913 that New Trier High School began its celebrated history with the Suburban League. The marching band was a big part of the excitement. (Courtesy of New Trier High School.)

In 1931, construction began on the desperately needed New Trier High School expansion. Because of the Great Depression, there was a shortfall in property tax revenues. Students volunteered to sell tax warrants door to door to help pay for this project. Students had shown similar initiative in World War I, having raised the money to purchase an ambulance for the Red Cross. (Courtesy of New Trier High School.)

These girls formed the 1934 girls' basketball team. New Trier High School provided many opportunities for girls to participate in sports compared to other high schools in the area. The girls' basketball Trevians' greatest rival has always been the Lady Wildkits of Evanston. (Courtesy of New Trier High School.)

North Shore Country Day School continued to thrive as a smaller, more personal alternative to New Trier and a more disciplined, rigorous alternative the Winnetka public schools. Still, North Shore Country Day School students had fun. Here a spirited game of tug-of-war takes place under the watchful eyes of teachers and of headmaster Perry Dunlap Smith. Behind them is the headmaster's residence, which faces Willow Road. (Courtesy of North Shore Country Day School.)

The North Shore Country Day School graduating class of 1936 wears white gowns and white summer dinner jackets, a tradition that continues to this day. That same year, New Trier High School would hand out a little over 500 diplomas. Both schools asked their students to don white dresses and white dinner jackets as well as bouquets and boutonnieres for the occasion. (Courtesy of North Shore Country Day School.)

Here is New Trier High School as it looked in the early 1940s. Students sold bonds to finance the purchase of a B-17 (the *Spirit of New Trier*) to aid the war effort, and also helped in the purchase of a B-29. One hundred and thirty-seven students and alumni were killed in World War II. (Courtesy of New Trier High School.)

In 1940, Crow Island School—a third elementary school—opened. It was designed by the father-son Finnish architectural team of Eliel and Eero Saarinen. Just like Hubbard Woods, the classrooms have their own outside entrances. Classes frequently explore the woods surrounding the school. Crow Island School was placed on the National Register of Historic Places in 1990. (Courtesy of Raymond Britt.)

Supt. Carleton Washburne left the Winnetka schools in 1943 to help with the reopening of schools and universities in Italy and take a position on the faculty of Brooklyn College, in 1949. Here he is pictured at his office in a thoughtful pose. In 1969, a junior high school named for Washburne was built—his influence on education in Winnetka remains profound. (Courtesy of the Winnetka Historical Society.)

Supt. Carleton Washburne's vision of developmental education remained in place long after he left. Here, in 1958, eighth grader Barry Fisher—a student in an accelerated Skokie School eighth-grade science class—studies the results of 20 years of Winnetka students' experiments with send-up balloons, charting their trajectory and eventual fall to earth. This sort of individual, student-led project would have made Superintendent Washburne very proud. (Courtesy of the Winnetka Historical Society.)

Winnetka elementary school students were well prepared for New Trier High School or whatever high school they attended. While taught a basic core curriculum, they were encouraged to become a "community of learners" who explored on their own. In 1952, a teacher demonstrates a math problem at Skokie School. All students would be expected to master the fundamentals of any such problem, but students who could study its implications would be encouraged. (Courtesy of the Winnetka Historical Society.)

In 1951, New Trier High School seemed like the perfect place to send a teenager for an education. Winnetka's population and prestige rose rapidly, as did the student enrollment at New Trier High School—projections suggested that the student population would swell to 3,500. In 1954, the original tower was torn down as part of a modernization effort to accommodate the influx of students. By the time construction began, it was already apparent that even the expansion would be inadequate. (Courtesy of New Trier High School.)

These New Trier High School students raise the flag on a 1953 morning, showing their patriotic spirit. In just 10 years, New Trier would reach its peak enrollment of over 6,600 students, requiring the opening of a second campus at Northfield. Enrollment would ebb so that the Northfield campus would be closed in 1981 but then reopened again in the 21st century. (Courtesy of New Trier High School.)

North Shore Country Day School limited its enrollment so as to ensure that its students had an experience much like a boarding school. This was in sharp contrast to Winnetka public schools and New Trier High School, both of which had seen its enrollment skyrocket in the 1950s. Here some students enjoy the spring afternoon on North Shore's campus. (Courtesy of North Shore Country Day School.)

North Shore Country Day School students participated in every level of campus life. In the mid-1960s, girls ring the morning bells announcing the beginning of the school day. Alumni Gilbert Fitzgerald remembers getting off the bus and racing with his classmates across the lawn to the headmaster's house where his golf cart was parked. Whoever reached the golf cart first had the pleasure of driving the headmaster across the field to his office. (Courtesy of North Shore Country Day School.)

The modern tower of New Trier High School was erected in 1954. The school was bursting at the seams, and the 27-acre campus was hemmed in at all sides. In the 1960s, a second campus was built in Northfield and named New Trier West High School. (Courtesy of New Trier High School.)

The New Trier High School graduating class of 2008 was given diplomas at Northwestern University's Welsh Ryan Arena because there is no place at the high school that can accommodate the large crowd of graduates and well-wishers. New Trier students outperform other Illinois high school students academically and are well prepared for the challenges they will face—97 percent of New Trier High School graduates go on to college. Note the white gowns on the girls and white summer dinner jackets on the boys—the uniform of graduation since the school's founding. (Courtesy of Raymond Britt.)

Education is not just for children. In 1915, Chicago high school teacher William A. Hadley became blind after a severe case of influenza. His doctor E. V. L. Brown suggested he teach himself braille. When a farmer's wife from Kansas wrote to Hadley to ask for his help in learning braille, he founded the Hadley School for the Blind together with Dr. Brown. It was designed as a correspondence school so that students could learn in their own homes. (Courtesy of the Hadley School for the Blind.)

Clarence Boyd Jones, Dr. Brown's son-in-law, was chairman of the Hadley School after Dr. Brown's death and began a capital campaign to move the school into its own building in 1957. Members of the Clarence Boyd Jones Society raise money to ensure that the school continues and expands its mission. (Courtesy of the Hadley School for the Blind.)

The Hadley School for the Blind groundbreaking was a celebration. The building is small compared to the work it accomplishes. It operates largely as a correspondence school, serving all 50 states and 90 countries and since its founding has never charged any student for its courses. In addition to teaching braille and other systems for the blind, the school offers a rigorous high school education and some college courses. Clarence Boyd Jones is seen in the second row, second from the left. (Courtesy of the Hadley School for the Blind.)

A community of learners requires the support of a good library. In 1910, the Winnetka Public Library was dedicated in memory of Henry Demarest Lloyd and his wife Jessie Bross Lloyd by their children. It was replaced by a modern building, seen here, in 1957. (Courtesy of the Winnetka Historical Society.)

A community of learners, dedicated to understanding their world and committed to their community, is exactly what Perry Dunlap Smith, Supt. Carleton Washburne, Fr. Frederick Haarth, and other learning leaders envisioned. Here, in the early 1980s, young Terry Brunner checks out books at the Winnetka Public Library. The library has expanded to create the Winnekta-Northfield Public Library District with a library in Winnetka and another in Northfield. (Courtesy of the Winnetka Historical Society.)

Three

SERVICE AND SACRIFICE

Winnetka was not yet incorporated when the Civil War broke out, but there is a record of two Winnetkan losses in battle—Charles Davis and George Willson (son of the village president who would be murdered 20 years later). Winnetka sent its sons and daughters into battle in subsequent wars. The price was high—in World War II alone, Winnetka lost 72 sons and one daughter. And sacrifice was continued at home. New Trier students sold bonds during World War II to finance the purchase of a B-17 (the *Spirit of New Trier*) to aid the war effort and help in the purchase of a B-29. Food rationing created challenges for the housewives who turned their flower gardens into victory gardens.

There are ways to sacrifice for a community in peacetime. Winnetkans join clubs and volunteer their services to help others in their community and around the world. The village is home to philanthropists who can write a check as well as folks who quietly volunteer their time at the schools, the churches, in the city, and overseas.

Albert Banfield Capron enlisted as a corporal in the 33rd Illinois Infantry at the outbreak of the Civil War. He later was transferred as a captain to the 11th Cavalry under his father's command and was elevated to the rank of colonel. He returned to Winnetka and raised three children—Horace, Bert, and Florence—and died of pneumonia in 1890. There were so many Capron family members in the military that they were collectively known as the "Fighting Caprons." (Courtesy of the Winnetka Historical Society.)

Julian Buckbee had been a member of the Winnetka Cadet Corps before he signed on for service in the Spanish-American War. His father attained the rank of colonel in the Civil War. In commemoration of Buckbee's service, two cannons from the Spanish-American War were installed in the Winnetka Village Green. (Courtesy of the Winnetka Historical Society.)

Dr. Alice Barlow Brown was the first female doctor in town and was a founder of the Winnetka Woman's Club. At the start of World War I, she attempted to join the U.S. Army Medical Reserve Corps. Denied entry because she was a woman, she was instrumental in the creation of the American Women's Hospital Service. While stationed in France, she wrote letters to her Winnetka friends asking for help in purchasing an ambulance. She served in France, Serbia, and China. (Courtesy of the Winnetka Historical Society.)

In 1918, 12 boys formed a "war club" at the Winnetka Community House in order to learn more about naval practices. Under the direction of Capt. Car Aspenwall and 1st Lt. Philip Eisendrath, the Junior Jackies quickly became one of the most popular boys' clubs. They made a formal offer to help the War Emergency Union—a nationwide women's group that put into place a civilian response plan. (Courtesy of the Winnetka Historical Society.)

Commonly called a "Jackie's Party," this get-together for navy yeomen at the Winnetka Community House allowed them some civilian company as a morale booster. Great Lakes Naval Training Station was just a few stops north on the Chicago & North Western Railroad line. (Courtesy of the Winnetka Historical Society.)

"It is an investment, not a loss when a man dies for his country," 2nd Lt. Dinsmore Ely wrote to his family just before his death in an aerial fight over Villacoublay, France, during World War I. A fierce member of the Lafayette Flying Corps, Dinsmore was only 24 years old. (Courtesy of the Winnetka Historical Society.)

Second Lt. Dinsmore Ely was buried at Versailles, France, with great honor from the French—he had served in the U.S. Army as a member of the French Corps. His father, Dr. James O. Ely, collected his letters and papers to publish in 1919 as *Dinsmore Ely: One Who Served*. The book was immensely popular. (Courtesy of the Winnetka Historical Society.)

"IT IS AN INVESTMENT NOT A LOSS
WHEN A MAN DIES FOR HIS COVNTRY"

DINSMORE ELY
1894 —————— 1918

* LAFAYETTE FLYING CORPS *
2ND LIEUT AIR SERVICE S.C.U.S.A.
* * FELL AT VILLACOUBLAY * *
BURIED CIMETIERE DES GONARDS
* * VERSAILLES * * FRANCE * *

In response to the book's popularity, plans were made to design an appropriate memorial in Winnetka. This is a drawing of what was proposed as appropriately grateful for his investment. The cenotaph was designed by Samuel Otis, son of William Otis, and completed in 1927. Second Lt. Dinsmore Ely's observation about the nature of investment and loss is inscribed at its base. (Courtesy of the Winnetka Historical Society.)

73

The cenotaph was built at the western edge of the Winnetka Village Green, at the top of a gently sloping lawn. Ten Winnetka names—sons who had died during World War I—were inscribed on its surface as well as those who have perished in later wars and conflicts. Although the hope has always been that no new names would ever have to be added, that has not proved the case. (Courtesy of the Winnetka Historical Society.)

Architect Samuel Otis served as an officer in the U.S. Navy Reserve during World War I, in command of a submarine chaser off the coast of England. He became active in Winnetka's American Legion post, and it was his job to call the roll of the dead at Memorial Day services at the cenotaph he designed. Here is a photograph of him "conferring with the war council" (looking in a double mirror) in 1918. In 1986, he drowned in Lake Michigan under suspicious circumstances. (Courtesy of the Winnetka Historical Society.)

The cenotaph has become the central location of solemn rituals at Memorial Day and the Fourth of July. This Memorial Day service in 1930 would have brought back memories to the men and women who served during World War I. (Courtesy of the Winnetka Historical Society.)

Winnetka sent many of its sons to serve in the armed forces during World War II. But it also sent its women, and it lost one daughter—Millicent Yates—in 1944 in a U.S. Army ambulance accident in Italy. Here a proud Sallie Ellen Welsh, a debutante of 1941, poses for her official portrait as an ensign for the WAVES. Walsh ultimately came home to marry Wilson Van Arsdale and raised a family. (Courtesy of the Winnetka Historical Society.)

This spring 1944 parade was a rousing send-off to troops leaving for World War II. During the war, there were many sacrifices. Every available piece of metal was melted down in order to help build tanks, ships, aircraft, and munitions. One of two cannons on the Winnetka Village Green commemorating the Spanish-American War was melted down. The other was hidden by architect Samuel Otis in his closet and only brought out again after the war was over. (Courtesy of the Winnetka Historical Society.)

Even during peacetime, Winnetkans recognize their duty to serve. Donald Henry Wagener joined the U.S. Navy in 1949. He trained as a communications specialist at Naval Station Great Lakes in North Chicago, Illinois. He is pictured here at work on maneuvers in the Caribbean Sea that same year. He returned home to raise a family in Winnetka. (Courtesy of the Budinger-Wagener family.)

A career soldier's return home is always met with gratitude. Here John McCoy poses with his family in 1945. Winnetkans have served in every major conflict, including the two Persian Gulf wars. Officers from the Naval Station Great Lakes and the now-closed Naval Air Station Glenview have made their home in Winnetka. (Courtesy of the Winnetka Historical Society.)

There are other ways to serve than in the armed forces. Winnetkans have generous hearts, and they like to come together in the spirit of friendship and service. Nowhere is that seen more clearly than in the Winnetka Rotary Club, founded in 1924. Rotarians from Winnetka have worked on service projects in such far-flung places as India, Uganda, and Cuba. Here Rotarians and the wives celebrate at their fund-raising dinner in 1928 at Matz Hall in the Winnetka Community House. (Courtesy of the Winnetka Historical Society.)

Philanthropy does not always have to leave the village limits. In 1923, the Winnetka Chamber of Commerce was established to help promote local businesses. Because Winnetka is blocked from furthering its boundaries, the vitality of local businesses is particularly acute in maintaining a stable tax base. These Winnetka Chamber of Commerce members and spouses dine at a fund-raiser in the late 1920s at Matz Hall in the Winnetka Community House. (Courtesy of the Winnetka Historical Society.)

The Winnetka Preparedness Club brought together community leaders to devise plans for natural disasters and wartime emergencies. At a club fund-raiser in 1925, members stop mid-festivities for a picture. (Courtesy of the Winnetka Historical Society.)

The Lions Club of Winnetka is a benefactor to the Hadley School for the Blind. Bring the Blind a Bit of Light Broom Sale was an annual event in the 1940s and 1950s. Service clubs have played an important part in helping Winnetkans maintain strong friendships. (Courtesy of the Winnetka Historical Society.)

The Winnetka Community House has always lived up to its motto as "the place where community happens." Clubs, classes, meetings, theatrical productions—yes, but there has always been a feeling that one can simply sit for a spell. Here the front hallway is decorated for Christmas 1929. (Courtesy of the Winnetka Historical Society.)

Winnetka neighborhood circle groups formed by Cora Davies in 1914 helped newly arriving women get acquainted with their community. These women paused for a picture at a 1920 costume party hosted by the Hawthorne Lane Circle. Neighborhood circles still exist today. (Courtesy of the Winnetka Historical Society.)

Being a debutante has become associated with a life of luxury and ease, but in actuality, debutantes were and are required to do a significant amount of charitable and fund-raising work during their coming-out year. Virginia Beaupre Miller poses with her parents before the Presentation Ball in 1932. Winnetka still has a Fortnightly Club, which presents debutantes to the community. (Courtesy of the Winnetka Historical Society.)

Boy Scouts practice semaphore training in the gymnasium at the Winnetka Community House. The first Boy Scout troop in Winnetka was formed in 1915 and concentrated its efforts on its drum and bugle corps, raising animals, public safety and signaling in both semaphore and Morse code. (Courtesy of the Winnetka Historical Society.)

Campfire Girls practice first aid on a hapless young man under the watchful eye of their leaders. The Campfire Girls met at the Winnetka Community House and, in their early years, focused on relief efforts for the needy as well as emergency preparedness. (Courtesy of the Winnetka Historical Society.)

Winnetka children were well aware of the need to think of the community at large and to think of the sacrifices necessary for others. These children, in a public school play in the early 1940s, stress the need for food rationing and for food conservation. (Courtesy of the Winnetka Historical Society.)

Christ Church
Winnetka, Ill.

Churches provide an opportunity for worship, service, and sacrifice for the community. The original Christ Church was built in 1869 by John Garland in memory of his wife Susannah. The church was open to all denominations, but Garland gave the church and land to the Episcopal Church in honor of his fourth wife, Juliette. The current Christ Church was built in 1904 in memory of Emilie Hoyt Fox and her three children, who died in the Iroquois Theater fire. Members can worship at the original church on Sheridan Road or the chapel at Oak Street and Maple Avenue. (Courtesy of the Winnetka Historical Society.)

The Winnetka Congregational Church originally held its services in the vacated one-room Unitarian church at the corner of Cherry Street and Maple Avenue. Twenty-two members attended the first services in 1874. (Courtesy of the Winnetka Historical Society.)

The Winnetka Congregational Church Sunday school class of seventh graders in the early 1900s utilizes a screen to separate the girls and boys. The boys must have worked harder at their studies because their teacher was seated with them, while some of the girls had a chance to daydream. Rev. James William Frederick Davies became director of the religious education in 1909, and it is he who formulated the idea of the Winnetka Community House. (Courtesy of the Winnetka Historical Society.)

The Winnetka Congregational Church dedicated its Pine Street house of worship in 1936. In 1957, it withdrew from its congregational affiliation to become a community church, affirmed by its motto inscribed over the doors to the church—A House of Worship for All People. Its women's society has held an annual rummage sale since 1902, the proceeds of which are distributed to charitable organizations associated with the church. (Courtesy of the Winnetka Historical Society.)

Sacred Heart Church in the Hubbard Woods neighborhood serves both Winnetka and Glencoe Catholics. It was founded in 1897 by Fr. Frederick Haarth, and its modest first building was replaced in 1925 with its present-day structure. (Courtesy of the Winnetka Historical Society.)

Although the First Church of Christ, Scientist was founded in 1924, it was not until 1941 when that the current church, designed by Spencer S. Beman, was dedicated. The church maintains a reading room at 804 Elm Street. There is no clergy—members are elected to three-year terms as readers for services on Sundays. (Courtesy of the Winnetka Historical Society.)

SS. Faith, Hope and Charity Catholic Church on the south side of the village first encountered initial resistance, perhaps because the temperance-minded Protestants clashed with the beer-drinking German Catholics. In 1936, the Alles family—originally from Germany—donated three and a half acres near the Indian Hill Club for the creation of the parish. The village fought the transfer, and the issue was ultimately decided by the Supreme Court. That year, the first mass was said at New Trier Auditorium with 375 people in attendance. (Courtesy of Raymond Britt.)

SS. Faith, Hope and Charity Catholic Church was dedicated in 1962 and is rich in symbolism in its every aspect. The angels trumpet the good news of the Gospel from the spire atop the church. A rectory, a parish school, a gymnasium, and a small chapel are on the church's grounds. (Courtesy of Raymond Britt.)

There is service and sacrifice in the profession of being a policeman or fireman. At the village yards, from left to right, officers Raymond Nelson, Robert Smith, W. Lincoln Rogers, and Paul Herklotz practice their firearms skills. The police department works hard to maintain a low crime rate in Winnetka, and the village is widely regarded as among the safest on the North Shore. (Courtesy of the Winnetka Police Department.)

Police have also served as liaisons to the wider community. Here Lt. Robert Martin explains fingerprinting to two Boy Scouts in 1964. Police officers teach drug education and bicycle safety in the schools and maintain two service officers at New Trier High School. (Courtesy of the Winnetka Police Department.)

While the main occupation of the fire department is to extinguish fires, the Winnetka Fire Department also provides advanced life support and ambulance service, underwater dive and rescue operations, and public education. (Courtesy of the Winnetka Police Department.)

The police and fire departments work closely with the Coast Guard in emergencies that take place on Lake Michigan. (Courtesy of the Winnetka Police Department.)

At a routine traffic stop in May 1957, patrolman Robert E. Burke, pictured here behind the police station on Green Bay Road, was shot by a driver as he returned to the vehicle with the driver's license. He is the town's only officer killed in the line of duty. (Courtesy of the Winnetka Police Department.)

Four

WINNETKANS HAVE FUN

With sacrifice and service as its cornerstone, one might get the impression that Winnetkans are a dour lot. Nothing could be further from the truth. Winnetkans are a boisterous, fun-loving group of people. Whether it is a pickup game of basketball at the courts outside Washburne Junior High School or an organized paddle tennis league at the Nielsen Tennis Center, Winnetkans are good sports. And they have plenty of activities all year long—the town boasts two beautiful golf courses, seven beaches, indoor and outdoor tennis courts, a baseball field, a forest preserve, and several kid-friendly parks. The Winnetka Village Green is always busy with children playing tag, dogs chasing after the thrown ball, a pickup game of football, or an organized practice of a youth soccer game. There are also the planned events—the children's fair at the beginning of summer, six o'clock caroling on Christmas Eve, and the Memorial Day and Fourth of July solemnities.

The notion of a village entity in charge of parks and recreation was first discussed at a village meeting in 1893. T. S. Dick (who would go on to be village president in 1894) presented a paper on the Winnetka Village Green, other parks, the beaches, and the forests of the village. He argued that these spaces should be preserved and protected for the use of all Winnetka. Based on his suggestions, a park district was formed 10 years later, and its first commissioners were picked at the annual town meeting.

For many years, the Winnetka Woman's Club sponsored a Shakespeare festival on the Winnetka Village Green. In the spring of 1916, Betty Rogers prepares for her role in *A Midsummer Night's Dream* with her train carried by Marian Montgomery. (Courtesy of the Winnetka Historical Society.)

This 1916 Fourth of July children's tableau commemorates the peace between the pioneers and the Native Americans as part of the story of the country's origins. The story concludes with the gratitude of the community for the sacrifices of its forebears. (Courtesy of the Winnetka Historical Society.)

Camp Douglas Smith, named for the first major donor to the Winnetka Community House, was a gift from his son Kenneth Smith in the mid-1930s. Located on Hamlin Lake, near Ludington, Michigan, the camp was organized in four-week sessions for boys, girls, and families from Winnetka. The girls' camp was generally scheduled at the beginning of the summer, on the assumption that girls were less daunted by the chill and rain that usually opened the season. In 1983, the camp was sold to the family of John Modjeski, longtime caretaker of the camp. (Courtesy of the Winnetka Historical Society.)

The original clubhouse for the Winnetka Park District, pictured here in 1934, has long since been torn down to make way for the Nielsen Tennis Center and Winnetka Park District offices. (Courtesy of the Winnetka Park District.)

In 1946, Winnetka residents Arthur C. Nielsen Sr., Barbara Nielsen Whitcomb, and Arthur C. Nielsen Jr. celebrate the two men's victory at the United States Father and Son Tennis Championship, which they would again win in 1948. The elder Nielsen created the National Radio Index in 1942 and, later, the Nielsen television ratings system in order to gauge audience response to media. The family made a significant donation to the Winnetka Park District for the creation of the Nielsen Tennis Center and the concomitant Winnetka Park District offices. (Courtesy of the Winnetka Park District.)

Every year, the Fourth of July festivities include races across the Winnetka Village Green. Boys and girls, and men and women, divided into age groups, compete for prizes. There is even a family relay race. The races are sponsored by the Winnetka Park District as part of daylong festivities that begin with the races on the Winnetka Village Green and end with late-night fireworks at Duke Childs Field. Here, in 1947, recently retired village engineer Frank Windes awards first place to a delighted and exuberant young man. (Courtesy of the Winnetka Park District.)

New Trier High School relies heavily on the Winnetka Park District for use of its facilities and parks. Here the school's field hockey team practices in the Skokie Playfields on the west edge of town in 1948. The clubhouse in the background was torn down to make way for the Nielsen Tennis Center. (Courtesy of the Winnetka Park District.)

The Winnetka Park District golf course was opened in 1917 as a 2,455-yard, nine-hole course designed by W. H. Langford. One year later, the nine remaining holes were added. The golf club maintains a driving range and a par-three golf course. In 1966, this golfer at the seventh tee does not mind the distraction of a lawn mower directly behind him. (Courtesy of the Winnetka Park District.)

Golf instruction starts early for Winnetka children. The town has two golf courses—the Winnetka Park District course and the Indian Hill Club course. New Trier High School's girls' and boys' golf teams both use the Winnetka Park District course. Here a clubhouse professional gives a lesson. (Courtesy of the Winnetka Park District.)

Winnetka Park District employees, from left to right, Ray Runnfeldt, Kae Stetzel, and George Caskey admire golfer Chick Evans's swing. Caskey worked at the Winnetka Park District from 1937 to 1967, ending his career as superintendent. In 1916, Chick Evans was the first to win both the U.S. Open and the U.S. Amateurs tournaments in one year. He competed in over 50 amateur golf tournaments and created a scholarship program for golf caddies. (Courtesy of the Winnetka Park District.)

In 1953, these hockey players skate at the outdoor rink in Indian Hill Park. The original name for the hockey program was the Win-field Hockey Association, in recognition of the members of its teams who were from the neighboring town of Northfield. This name was changed to the Winnetka Hockey Program after a visiting team arrived in Winfield, Illinois, and was baffled to discover it had gone to the wrong place. (Courtesy of the Winnetka Park District.)

Every winter, the Winnetka Park District creates outdoor rinks at Indian Hill Park and at the Hubbard Woods playfield. This skater is enjoying a cold but cheery skate—behind her is the warming house at Hubbard Woods. The skate park and warming house were featured in the 1990 film *Home Alone*. (Courtesy of the Winnetka Historical Society.)

Onetime village marshal Theodore Flynn finished his career with the Winnetka Police Department as a parks patrol officer. He was known for loving a good cigar and was so seldom seen without one that this is an unusual picture for that reason. (Courtesy of the Winnetka Park District.)

Winnetka boasts beautiful public beaches at Elder Lane, Maple Street, and Lloyd and Tower Roads as well as Centennial Beach, which is reserved for use by dogs and their owners. Here, in 1962, residents frolic at the Tower Road beach. (Courtesy of the Winnetka Park District.)

In 1958, these boys race cars they built using old lawn mower engines. Because of safety issues, the races have been discontinued, and instead of roaring engines, the neighbors are awakened on Saturday mornings with the sounds of children playing in the American Youth Soccer Organization games. This park was named the Nick Corwin Park to honor the second grader who lost his life when Laurie Dann attacked students at Hubbard Woods School. (Courtesy of the Winnetka Park District.)

When the schools declare a snow day, it is only natural to head for the hills—the hill at Skokie Playfields, that is! In 1966, these carefree children brought out their toboggan. The toboggan slides have since been removed because of safety concerns, but children still sled on the hills whenever there is a good dusting of snow. (Courtesy of the Winnetka Park District.)

A mother and child take a gentler, more leisurely slide down the hill at Skokie Playfields. The Skokie Playfields is part of a Winnetka Park District complex that includes the Nielsen Tennis Center, the Winnetka Park District offices, the golf course, an indoor ice arena, and fields for soccer, lacrosse, baseball, and football. (Courtesy of the Winnetka Park District.)

In 1972, a group of hockey parents were successful in raising over $600,000 to build Winnetka's indoor ice arena. In 1975, the first annual ice show was performed—these skaters are pictured rehearsing their moves. Olympic figure skater Nicole Bobek trained at the arena, as did Sarah Tueting, the Olympic gold medal hockey player who had trained with the New Trier hockey club. (Courtesy of the Winnetka Park District.)

On the Saturday before Easter Sunday, the Winnetka Park District sponsors an egg hunt at the West Elm Street Park. Plastic eggs are filled with candy or slips of paper to be turned in for prizes. The Easter Bunny makes an appearance. (Courtesy of the Winnetka Park District.)

The morning parade on the Fourth of July is a participatory exercise in a daylong celebration that concludes with fireworks at Duke Childs Field. It is a day of contradictions—exuberance, solemn remembrance, gratitude to those who have served their country, and awe at the explosions in the night sky. Here a family brings its own playful sensibilities to a 1973 parade. (Courtesy of the Winnetka Park District.)

Sometimes fun can be a solitary venture. Here Winnetka resident Jay Collins casts his line for fish at the Tower Road beach. On any summer day, one can find fishermen whiling away their time at the beaches or at the Skokie Lagoons. (Courtesy of the Winnetka Historical Society.)

In June, the board of the Winnetka Community Nursery School sponsors a two-day children's fair. On the last day of school, children race from their classrooms to the Winnetka Village Green for rides, face painting, cotton candy, and games. The cenotaph becomes a central location for missing parents to find their children and for raffle prizes to be handed out. It is the measure of the investment that Dinsmore Ely and his fellow patriots made so that Winnetka children can have such fun. (Courtesy of Raymond Britt.)

Five

ACHIEVEMENT AND INNOVATION

Winnetka is the hometown of many celebrated individuals—publisher Henry Demarest Lloyd and his son Henry Bross, Secretary of Transportation Samuel Skinner and Secretary of Defense Donald Rumsfeld, stars Rock Hudson and Chris O'Donnell, and the band members of Fall Out Boy. Winnetka is a place of innovation and independence—Winnetka educational pioneers and the pioneers in creating the caucus system of government were matched by pioneers in engineering and design.

Nowhere was the Winnetka spirit of innovation more apparent than in its curmudgeonly citizen Harold L. Ickes. Ickes served as secretary of the interior under Pres. Franklin D. Roosevelt, and while much can be written about his impact on the country as a whole, in Winnetka he transformed the community in two ways: the public works project to create the Skokie Lagoons and the railroad track depression project.

Independent thinking has always been encouraged in Winnetka. If one wants evidence that Winnetkans are innovators, one need look no further than Frank Whitney, who, with childlike enthusiasm, invented and patented a device that turned an ordinary bicycle into a bicycle built for two. (Courtesy of the Winnetka Historical Society.)

In 1896, when Whitney patented his invention, tandem bicycles were quite popular. His tandem attachment allowed for both riders to do their own pedaling. Here he demonstrates the bicycle, riding behind his friend Carson Hood in front of the Whitney home on Linden Avenue. (Courtesy of the Winnetka Historical Society.)

In the 19th century, Winnetka homes had their own wells, like this one at the Schackford home at 594 Elm Street. In 1893, Winnetka became one of the first villages to own its own utilities, with the building of the water tower at the Tower Road beach. Visitors to the tower were allowed to climb the stairs to the viewer's platform where they had a grand view of the village. (Courtesy of the Winnetka Historical Society.)

In 1972, high-pressure pumps made the tower superfluous, and when the need arose for tuck-pointing, village trustees decided to tear down the tower instead. This exposed the previously hidden smokestack of the village's electrical plant. Some Winnetkans mistakenly believe the smokestack is the water tower. (Courtesy of the Winnetka Historical Society.)

In 1900, the municipal electrical plant was built, joining the waterworks at the Tower Road beach. The first electrical lights were installed at Academy Hall, and the gaslights were lowered and the electric lights fired up to great applause from the crowd that had gathered. The plant is now part of the Illinois Municipal Electric Agency but, at a moment's notice, can power up for the village. On September 11, 2001, the village was temporarily taken off the national power grid in order to ensure reliable service. (Courtesy of the Winnetka Historical Society.)

The west side of town was once a flooded plain, which in summer became a breeding ground for disease-bearing mosquitoes. In 1927, members of the Mosquito Abatement Committee met with state officials to try to find a solution. From left to right, Mosquito Abatement Committee members Morris L. Greeley, Charles O. Schneider, and Rev. James William Frederick Davies are shown by the unidentified expert (second from right) how to use ladles to cull standing water so that the mosquito population could be counted. Village engineer Frank Windes (right) looks on. (Courtesy of the Winnetka Historical Society.)

His 1943 autobiography was titled *Autobiography of a Curmudgeon*, and Harold L. Ickes fit that description. Independent, combative, arrogant—he was all these things. But Ickes was also a person with a great love of Winnetka. He was appointed to Pres. Franklin D. Roosevelt's cabinet as secretary of the interior in 1933. His son would work for the Clinton administration. (Courtesy of the Winnetka Historical Society.)

At the urging of Secretary of the Interior Harold L. Ickes, the revolutionary project to move standing water away from the village was begun. In 1933, Lt. T. C. Shanahan, Maj. C. A. Chapman, and Capt. W. F. MacGill, from left to right, reported for duty in Winnetka. (Courtesy of the Winnetka Historical Society.)

The Skokie Lagoons project was a 10-year undertaking: 1,000 Civilian Conservation Corps workers created seven lagoons, five dams, and two drainage ditches out of what had been a swamp on the west edge of town. This innovative and ambitious undertaking created more available land for Winnetka and relieved the mosquito problem. (Courtesy of the Winnetka Historical Society.)

In 1938, Sibyl Brittain and Janet Getgood were killed when a train struck the car in which they were driving as they returned home from helping out at a children's Halloween party at the Winnetka Community House. Thirty-eight other people had lost their lives in such a way, but the deaths of the two women galvanized the town, particularly because Janet's husband George was director of the Winnetka Community House. Harold L. Ickes immediately proposed a second major public works project—the lowering of the railroad tracks. After completion of the project, these commuters walk down a staircase to the lowered train platform at the Winnetka station. (Courtesy of the Winnetka Historical Society.)

The $15 million train depression project called for street crossings to be replaced with bridges over the passing trains. Seven bridges were built to replace the crossings, including one connecting east and west Scott Avenue. (Courtesy of the Winnetka Historical Society.)

Instead of a railroad crossing, Elm Street between Lincoln Avenue and Green Bay Road is a bucolic bridge with faux gaslights and limestone guardrails. The bridge has been named the Windes Bridge in honor of Frank Windes. (Courtesy of the Winnetka Historical Society.)

From its first days, the Winnetka Police Department has kept up with the latest technology and innovations. In 1929, three officers—from left to right, John Luensman, LaVerne Halbert, and Lester Baker—tool around on their brand-new Harley-Davidson motorcycles. They were dubbed the "Eagles of the Road" and could catch up with even the speediest car. (Courtesy of the Winnetka Police Department.)

In 1954, Lt. Frank Berkenheier demonstrates a brand-new devise that aided in catching speeders. It utilized a trip wire laid across the road. The trip wire does not appear to be all that different from the rope strung across the road by village marshal Henry Leach and officer John Dehmlous when the first cars were bought in Winnetka. (Courtesy of the Winnetka Police Department.)

Officers Joseph Sumner, John Keil, Patricia Weymueller, and Chris Benz are at work at the police department communications center. Today the Winnetka Police Department has cameras in strategic locations around the village to allow the communications center to respond quickly to emergencies. In the event of an emergency at New Trier High School, the communications center is able to access cameras at every hallway that would allow real-time imaging of the school's interior. (Courtesy of the Winnetka Police Department.)

Six

A BEAUTIFUL LAND

Winnetka was once a place to stop off on the way to someplace else. But now it is a place to stay, to make a home, to raise children. It is the American ideal of a small town but with access to the city that is just a few steps to the train station or a quick drive to the expressway. Winnetka has been immortalized and idealized in such movies as *Home Alone, Ferris Bueller's Day Off, Uncle Buck,* and *Sixteen Candles* and the television series *Winnetka Road, Sisters,* and *Swingtown.*

Winnetka is a wonderful place to raise a family. Here Francis J. Budinger celebrates Father's Day 1942 with his children. This picture was the cover of the *Winnetka Talk* newspaper for that week. Budinger later became president of the Franklin Life Insurance Company. (Courtesy of the Budinger-Wagener family.)

Winnetkans are accustomed to friendly, courteous service. Lakeside Foods opened in 1958, and its owner Joseph Smith (far right) made the small grocery a place where the customer is given the "red carpet treatment." Even today, baggers carry groceries to the car and customers can arrange for home delivery. House charges are allowed, as they are at many village stores. Here "Little Oscar" from the Oscar Mayer Company pays a visit to Lakeside Foods at its grand opening. (Courtesy of Lakeside Foods.)

The architecture of the commercial district has not changed much since William Otis, Edwin Clark, and Sam Otis were in their prime. In 1968, the corner of Elm and Chestnut Streets housed a fashionable department store. The corner looks much the same today, with a real estate office using the space. (Courtesy of the Winnetka Police Department.)

Winnetkans can often count the generations of their family that have lived in town. It is a source of pride and distinction. Florence Henderson Matz married Rudolph Matz in November 1890. The couple was instrumental in the creation of the Winnetka Community House, and Matz Hall, the theater, is named for them. (Courtesy of the Winnetka Historical Society.)

In 1946, when Matz's granddaughter Charlotte Boyd married Willard McNitt Jr., she wore the very same wedding dress. The McNitts made their home in Winnetka, and their adult children remained in the community as well. (Courtesy of the Winnetka Historical Society.)

In 1990, this house on Lincoln Avenue became the most recognized building in Winnetka. Director John Hughes used this Georgian Revival as home to the hapless McCallister family that left son Kevin at home in *Home Alone* and *Home Alone 2*. (Courtesy of Raymond Britt.)

This lakefront Spanish Revival house is best known for being home to insurance entrepreneur W. Clement Stone and his wife. It was built by Lena Gilmore, a wealthy widow, in 1912. The third-floor ballroom was used for many wonderful parties, including the debut of Gilmore's niece Isabel in 1916. Winnetka has many large and beautiful homes, often shielded from the gaze of passersby with gates or arbor vitae. (Courtesy of Joseph Presser.)

In 2003, the historical society moved the Schmidt-Burnham cabin from Tower Road to the woods outside Crow Island School. Although the house required some repairs, it is available for tours and is a beloved link to Winnetka's past. (Courtesy of Raymond Britt.)

A wedding carriage brings guests from the chapel to the reception, and it carries an optimistic banner—"Our first ones will be Twins." The beautiful Victorian home behind this carriage was donated to the Winnetka Historical Society. It is the society's first permanent home and serves as both museum and office space. (Courtesy of the Winnetka Historical Society.)

When Zernah Patterson came to Winnetka, she could not have realized what a legacy she would leave just by running a tavern for weary travelers to stop on their way to someplace else. In her last years, she lived with her son Joseph's children. She died in 1874 and is buried with her daughter and son-in-law in the Morgan Burdick plot at Forest Home Cemetery in Milwaukee. (Courtesy of the Winnetka Historical Society.)

If one walks out onto the Skokie Lagoons, one is scarcely aware that the landscape has been molded and created by man. Instead, one thinks of the how Winnetka might have been when the Potawatomi migrated through or when the Patterson family arrived. It was, and is now, a beautiful land. (Courtesy of Raymond Britt.)

Visit us at
arcadiapublishing.com